THE WAY OUT OF DEPRESSION

Do Life Like a Boss

EDWARDS DIVINELOVE

ISBN: 9798849373898

DEDICATION

This book is dedicated to my Life Coach, Rev. Dr. Chris Oyakhilome..

CONTENTS

INTRODUCTION

What is depression?

Depression is a state of the mind producing serious, long-term lowering of enjoyment of life or inability to visualize a happy future. Depression eats quite deep into the mind of the individual that is suffering from it.

It is very important to note that depression occurs in the mind, and as we all know our minds give us the enablement to relate with our world. The mind holds the power of thoughts, reasoning, imagination and interpretation. For instance, the reason that you are able to give meaning to what you are reading right now is because your mind is interpreting it to you.

It is also important to note that your mind gives interpretation based on the kind of training that it has received. We will shed more light on this moving forward.

Depression is a condition that makes those suffering from it emotionally and mentally weak, helpless and makes them lose a sense of direction in their lives. Most times it comes with a barrage of damaging thoughts of failure and insufficiency. Even worse, the victims report that they hear audible voices or see beings that tell them the most hurtful words. These thoughts or words may be related to the situations they are passing through at the time. For some others, nothing exactly might be the problem. In fact, they may have everything at their beck-and-call and have life moving on smoothly for them and yet keep stumbling down the road of depression. Many of them at one point start having very strong suicidal thoughts that even tend to further distort their seemingly shattered lives. These experiences make the victims feel like life is punishing them. They describe life as worthless and seem to take refuge in the assumption that they'll find the peace that they didn't find in life in death. Some of them think that they are punishing life or punishing their Creator, God by choosing to die instead of living; where in essence they are punishing their family members and loved ones.

The point is that they have the feeling of ending their consciousness. Unfortunately, consciousness doesn't end in death because the mind is not a part of the physical body. Death only opens one to a new environment with a new consciousness which may even be worse for the person involved. Meanwhile, death is not really as cheap as many think it is. In the foregoing paragraph, I did mention that the mind is not a part of the physical body (or the brain as many would like to say). According to my life coach, Pastor Chris Oyakhilome (D.Sc. D.D), "The mind is the faculty of man's reasoning and thoughts. It holds the power of the imagination, recognition, and appreciation, and is responsible for processing feelings and emotions, resulting in attitudes and actions." Some people have made the mistake of thinking that the mind resides in the brain, but there is no scientific evidence supporting that.

The mind is an intangible spiritual entity and only the Word of God can shed the best light on it. In this book, I bring to you the way out of depression. The way out of depression is not death; certainly not. You are not hated by God—or life. You are a special person made in God's image and for God's pleasure. You are not supposed to be depressed—yes, you heard me right. You deserve more than wallowing in self-pity. You have a reason for living. There's a purpose for your life and you have to fulfill it. It is not the time to die. In fact, the very reason you thought to purchase and study a material like this is because you don't want to die but live. However, you do not just want to live; you want to live a happy and fulfilled life, waking up every day bubbling with new strength, fresh ideas, great dreams and great hopes for the future. You want to be on the top of your game; you want to do life like a boss. You want to win. You want to be happy. You want to be loved and appreciated. You want answers to your questions and the list goes on.

What if I told you that these things are possible? You might say, "Oh don't hand me that stuff! Do you how many therapy sessions I have been to? What have you to say that hasn't been heard? I just got this book because I want to give life the benefit of the doubt..." Well, in spite of what to you think, I still maintain that living an absolutely great life is possible and I have proved it several times. I will however advise that you keep an open mind and believe the truths that I am about to share with you. Sometimes what you may require for your healing may not even be answers to your questions but exposure to new information. The reason is that I am not just here help you come out of depression if you are depressed, but to help you learn how to effectively tame life's circumstances and do life like a boss. Enjoy the ride.

START WITH YOUR MIND

We established in the previous chapter that depression is a state of the mind. If that is true, as it is, it means that the problem is half-solved. The biggest part of a problem is, not knowing where the problem is coming from. If we detect where the problem is, it is only then that we can seek solution and in this case the problem is in the mind. Just before you say, "I have heard that before", keep reading. Now that you know that depression is a thing of the mind, what should you do with the information? It's very simple: just change your mind! I could just end this book here and be satisfied that I did a great job, because this is the solution! Nonetheless, I know that you'd like know how. If I don't tell you how, then this piece of information is useless to you.

I mentioned in the previous chapter that that your mind gives interpretation based on the kind of training that it has received. For instance, if your mind wasn't trained to read and understand English, this text would be meaningless to you. You may not even glance through it twice because it would be totally foreign to you. That's exactly what happens to you when you read a Chinese text especially if you have not being trained to read and understand Chinese. Perhaps the reason for your sadness and depression may be how your mind has been trained to respond to the situation you are going through. You will be amazed that someone else is going or has gone through that situation and came out unscathed. Why is that? It is because their minds have been trained to look at the situation differently.

It is not the situation that is destroying you, the wrong configuration of your mind is. The only way you can come out of depression and live that brilliant life that has only been in your dreams is through the reprogramming of your mind. God's Word says in Romans Chapter 12 verse 2: "And be not conformed to this world but be ye transformed by the renewing of your mind..." This means that it doesn't matter what you want you change, there's no better place to start than your mind. I believe that anyone who gets to know this should experience their light bulb moment! This is the secret that you need. However, if you decide to ignore this simple but powerful principle, you will do so at your own loss; and if you don't do something fast, the situation will get worse. I'm sure that's not what you want. It is just like a fire outbreak. When a fire outbreak starts and you don't control it, it will get worse and destroy a lot of properties and even lives.

When it comes to working on your mind, it may not be something that will be spontaneous like you taking a pill and waking up to realize that everything has changed. It will not happen that way; it will take some time. It reminds me of an old rhyme that goes:

Little by little say the thoughtful boy,
Moment by moment I will improve
Learning a little everyday...

Therefore, to make the lasting changes that you need to make, you must have a moment-by-moment improvement. That means you have to be consistent. After all, it took a long period of dwelling on negative thoughts to get you depressed. So you shouldn't expect to transform overnight, but one thing that is certain is that you will have the results if you are consistent.

How do I get the transformation? You may ask. Well, to answer that question, I will start by saying that the most important material to transform your life with is the Word of God that is enshrouded in the Bible.

Working on your mind does not require physical energy. Do not assume that you have become too tired to make a change. It is about disallowing and allowing the thoughts. You might say, "I cannot control my mind. I can't help but be sad." First, you have to understand that you are not a mind. You have a mind just the same way you have a hand. Your hands do not just raise themselves without your consent. You make use of them at will. In other words, you control them and not the other way round. The same goes for your mind. Take charge of your mind; don't be a slave of the wrong thoughts that come to your mind. Mount guard over your mind. Proverbs 4:23 in the Message Translation says, "Keep vigilant watch over your heart; that's where life starts".

If you didn't know, it is important to realize that life starts from your heart and therefore you are instructed to keep vigilant watch over it. The "heart" being referred to here is your human spirit and the door way to your spirit is your mind. If you would get the right things into your mind, you will start living the right life in the process of time. That suggests that you have a role to play in living a happier and fulfilling life because life does not begin from the outside, but from the inside. What you do to the inside reflects on the outside—that's where life begins. What if the wrong thoughts keep forcing themselves on you? Keep warding them off! You've got to keep practicing that until you become good at it. For God to ask you to keep vigilant watch, it means that there could be aggressors but you have the ability and the responsibility of getting rid of them because you own your mind. Therefore, OWN YOUR MIND! When the wrong thoughts come, the simple thing to do is to change your mind.

If you find yourself drifting back into such unwholesome thoughts, keep changing your mind. Think happy, fulfilling thoughts. There is no better material to think upon than God's Word--the Bible. It is important that you replace such bad thoughts with positive thoughts. That means, keep your mind busy with the right thoughts.

DEALING WITH THE SPIRITUAL

Have you ever heard someone say, "I have learnt how to live with my demons"? Live with your demons? How could you learn to live with demons? Do you know what demons are? It is sad that many people that make such statements do not understand what they say because they probably picked them up from their next door neighbor.

Demons are wicked, evil spirits who do nothing but destroy anything or anyone they come in contact with. You cannot live with them because they will destroy you. The Lord Jesus showed us how to deal and relate with demons in Mark 16:17 (Message Translation), "These are some signs that will accompany believers: They will THROW OUT DEMONS in my name..." Notice the words in uppercase. He enjoins us to throw out demons and not learn to manage them or live with them. The reality of demons is not a figment.

Demons are real spirits with personalities and they can either influence or control people to whom they gain access. Demons can launch their onslaughts through damaging thoughts, images, audible voices and experiences. There are conditions that certain folks find themselves in where they hear audible voices saying terrible, wicked and evil things to them. These people know more than everyone else that those voices are so real and sometimes even come with some evil force especially when the voices are giving them some instructions like asking them to commit suicide or murder. For some others, it may not be voices but some strong weighty thoughts that they can't seem to get rid of and that's how come they want to get rid of their minds via suicide. Many people go through these terrible experiences without knowing that they are caused by demons because demons are spirits and so, they do not have physical bodies but their influence cannot be denied. They can make people sad, unfulfilled and restless for no just cause. It is interesting that the Lord Jesus said that in His Name, we could throw out demons. As simple as that sounds, that could bring a lifelong mental health condition to an abrupt end. However, to be able to throw out demons, you must be the person that the Lord Jesus was referring to. He said, "These are some signs that will accompany believers..." The signs are for the people that believe and accept the Lordship of Jesus Christ in their lives.

I invite you to make Jesus Christ the Lord of your life by praying thus: "O Lord God, I believe with all my heart in Jesus Christ, Son of the living God. I believe He died for me and God raised Him from the dead. I believe He's alive today. I confess with my mouth that Jesus Christ is the Lord of my life from this day. Through Him and in His Name, I have eternal life; I'm born again. Thank you Lord, for saving my soul! I'm now a child of God. Hallelujah!"

Send me an e-mail to chibuonumdivinelove@gmail.com if you just said that prayer. Now, if you have been tormented by demons, you can simply say, "You demons of darkness I order you in the Name of Jesus to get out of my mind, get out of my body, and get out of my home, my business and my finances." Run devils out of your life in the Name of Jesus.

THE POWER OF THOUGHTS

First, what are thoughts?

Thoughts are pictures of the mind with constructive or destructive meaning. When the pictures of your mind are without meaning, then you are not thinking. Many people in life are prisoners of thoughts. They are in bondage to their minds.

The life you live today is the manifestation of the inner workings of your mind and that controls how people see and perceive you. It controls what happens to people when they come into your world. It doesn't matter what happens to you, what matters is if you have enough tools to deal with it. You are the character of your thoughts.

You can assume that people don't like you because of your social status or your ethnicity. You may have been through an abuse; you may have been raised to be afraid and so on. It doesn't matter what has happened to you, refuse to be in bondage to your mind. Have thoughts of hope. 1 Corinthians 13:13, "And now these three remain: faith, hope and love. But the greatest of these is love" (NIV). There are three "greats" but love is the greatest. Hope is great so stay hopeful, don't give up! And until know that you are loved, you will not make a success of your life.

Have confidence in the unconditional and unfailing love of God in Jesus Christ. He loves you personally. You are individually important to God and that was why He sent His Son, Jesus Christ to be a ransom for your sake about 2000 years ago. Maybe you are going through pains because of sickness; all you need to do is to believe that the Lord Jesus Christ paid for you. Even if it was your fault that you are facing that situation, He took responsibility for all your wrongs and errors and faults and died in your place. What punishment for sins or error can be worse than a capital punishment? He paid in full for ALL your errors; so you are not to blame! It is no longer your fault! That's good news!

Don't punish yourself or think that you are being punished for the wrong stuff you did because the Lord Jesus already took responsibility for all your errors. That should make you spring up on your feet and face life like a boss! All you need to do to activate this reality is believe in Jesus and declare Him to be the Lord of your life and salvation will be yours. It is only then that you will be absolved of all your faults and cast out demons that try to mess up your mind.

LIVE JOYFULLY

Jesus died to give us something. He came to give us life to enjoy. Enjoying your life doesn't mean going for a game show, going to the beach, taking a walk with friends. It means enjoying every moment, enjoying where you are, what you are doing—whether you are working or playing. Take pride in yourself because you are a child of God and God is fulfilling His dreams through you. You also have to realize that we are not all the same and we may not approach life the same way. What is strenuous to someone may be easy for another. Be happy with yourself. The fact that you are not exactly like someone else and you not putting in as much effort as someone else does not mean that something is wrong with you. Accept yourself. Until you learn to accept yourself, you cannot make any improvement on yourself. We should make improvements; we should grow. 2 Peter 3:18 (MSG) says, "Grow in grace and understanding of our Master and Savior, Jesus Christ. Glory to the Master, now and forever! Yes!"

Growth is like a journey, and while you are on the journey, you can enjoy the process rather than getting frustrated because of what you couldn't do at a particular time. Whatever you do to add to your progress shouldn't be done out of frustration. Relish the moment. Don't be too hard on yourself. "Therefore take no thought, saying, What shall we eat? or, What shall we drink? or, Wherewithal shall we be clothed? (For after all these things do the Gentiles seek:) for your heavenly Father knoweth that ye have need of all these things" (Matthew 6:31-32). Why should anyone read this and still fret about anything in life? The one who has told you not to worry about tomorrow is the owner of tomorrow; He's aware that everything you require for an excellent life has already been made available. So, refuse to be burdened with stress and anxiety. Don't worry about your work, family, business, finances, or anything.

Worry is fear in disguise. It is fear of negative possibilities; the imminence of unwanted outcomes. Fear attracts its images. If you keep worrying about getting sick, for example, soon enough, you'll fall sick. The cure for worrying is living in God's Word. Jesus said, "Come unto me, all ye that labour and are heavy laden, and I will give you rest. Take my yoke upon you, and learn of me; for I am meek and lowly in heart: and ye shall find rest unto your souls. For my yoke is easy and my burden is light". (Matthew 11:28-30). Philippians 4:6 says, "Be careful for nothing; but in everything by prayer and supplication with thanksgiving let your requests be made known unto God." Act on the Word. Rather than worry, receive whatever you require, and live in the consciousness of Christ's victory, grace and abundant provisions.

Anything short of a life of absolute joy and fulfillment in Christ Jesus isn't God's best for you. Hebrews 4:3 says, "For we which have believed do enter into rest, as he said...." God finished all His works from the foundation of the world before He made man and rested from His works. That's the same life He's given us; a life free of struggles. Say this prayer: "Dear Father, thank you for dispelling every form of anxiety in my heart through the Word. I have already overcome Satan, the world and every crisis, being conscious that the greater One lives in me. I live in the peace and provisions of Christ. You've perfected all that concerns me. The peace of God which passes all understanding mantles my heart and mind, in Christ Jesus. Amen."

CONCLUSION

Thank you for studying this material. I hope it helped you a great deal. Everything I wrote here are things that I learnt from my Father, Life coach and Pastor, Rev. Dr. Chris Oyakhilome--some are even verbatim.

ABOUT THE AUTHOR

Edwards Divinelove is a trained Human Anatomist raised by a Pastor dad, a Psychologist mum and Pastor Chris. He has an insight into how mental health can be handled and managed, most especially through God's Word.

www.ingramcontent.com/pod-product-compliance
Lightning Source LLC
LaVergne TN
LVHW020545160826
845677LV00015B/4218

* 9 7 9 8 8 4 9 3 7 3 8 9 8 *